UNSHACKLED VOICES

INCARCERATED FATHERS SPEAK TO RESTORE THE FAMILY

By

YARAH & SAMUEL BEN ISRAEL

YARAH & SAMUEL BEN ISRAEL

Copyright © 2024 by Terri Jo Brown.

ISBN (paperback): 979-8-9907638-4-5

ISBN (hardcover): 979-8-9907638-5-2

All rights reserved. No part of this book may be reproduced or transmitted in any form or by any means, electronic or mechanical, including photocopying, recording, or by any information storage and retrieval system without express written permission from the author, except in the case of brief quotations embodied in critical reviews and certain other noncommercial uses permitted by copyright law.

Published in the United States of America by Lynx Publishers.

Preface

Restoring the Family: Heeding the Prophecy of Hosea 4:6

Introduction

In a society grappling with growing social challenges, we must heed the timeless wisdom found in the book of Hosea. The prophet's words ring true: "My people are destroyed for lack of knowledge" (Hosea 4:6, KJV). This profound statement serves as a clarion call, urging us to reflect on the root causes behind the crises plaguing our communities.

Far too often, we witness the devastating consequences of broken families and absent fathers. The Scriptures remind us, "Train up a child in the way he should go: and when he is old, he will not depart from it" (Proverbs 22:6, KJV). Yet, in too many instances, our children are deprived of the guidance, support, and love that a strong family structure provides.

As we examine the societal landscape, we are confronted with a sobering reality: the fabric of the American family has become unraveled, leaving a void that manifests in alarming ways. Our youth, yearning for purpose and direction, find themselves adrift, vulnerable to the lure of destructive paths.

However, within the darkest of circumstances, a glimmer of hope emerges. Through the powerful testimonies of incarcerated fathers who have found faith in Yahweh, we are reminded that even the most seemingly hopeless situations can be transformed by the power of redemption.

Restoring the Family: Biblical Insights and Incarcerated Fathers' Stories

1. The Story of Joseph and His Brothers (Genesis 37-50): This powerful narrative teaches us the importance of forgiveness, reconciliation, and the restoration of broken relationships. Despite the trials and tribulations Joseph faced, he ultimately forgave his brothers and reconciled with them, demonstrating the transformative power of love and understanding.

2. The Parable of the Prodigal Son (Luke 15:11-32): This beloved parable illuminates the themes of redemption, restoration, and the unconditional love of a father. Even when the son had strayed from the righteous path, the father's arms were open, welcoming him back with open arms. This story serves as a reminder of the power of forgiveness and the potential for transformation in the most broken of lives.

3. Incarcerated Fathers' Stories: In the pages of this book, you will find the inspiring stories of men who, like the prodigal son, have found their way back to Yahweh. These fathers, once entangled in the web of societal pitfalls, have experienced remarkable transformations, becoming Yahweh-fearing role models for their children and their communities. Their testimonies offer profound insights into the challenges faced by at-risk youth and provide practical solutions for breaking the cycle of dysfunction.

Embracing the Path Forward

As we strive to address the societal challenges we face, it is imperative that we turn our attention to the foundational unit of society: the family. By championing the importance of fatherhood, fostering strong family bonds, and advocating for programs that support the rehabilitation and reintegration of individuals, we can begin to mend the fractured fabric of our communities.

Let us heed the call to reunite fathers and children, to restore the sacred ties that bind families together. In doing so, we can forge a path toward a future where every child is nurtured, empowered, and equipped to navigate the complexities of life with wisdom, resilience, and a deep connection to the timeless truths of the Scriptures.

Together, let us work towards a society where the family unit is strengthened, where fathers and children walk hand-in-hand, and where the transformative power of love and understanding becomes the cornerstone of our collective journey. Only then can we truly fulfill the prophecy of Hosea and usher in an era of hope, prosperity, and wholeness for all.

Table of Contents

Chapter 1: Hosea's Prophecy: The Clarion Call (Hosea 4:6) 3

Chapter 2: The Consequences of Ignorance - Learning from Biblical and Modern-Day Parallels 5

Chapter 3: The Unraveling of the American Family (Psalms 127:1) 7

Chapter 4: The Consequences of Fatherlessness (Proverbs 22:6) ... 10

Chapter 5: Restoring the Foundations: A Biblical Mandate (Psalms 11:3) 13

Chapter 6: The Testimony of Joseph: Forgiveness and Reconciliation (Genesis 37-50) 16

Chapter 7: The Parable of the Prodigal Son: Redemption (Luke 15:11-32) 21

Chapter 8: The Parable of the Prodigal Son: Restoration (Luke 15:11-32) 23

Chapter 9: From Darkness to Light - An Incarcerated Father's Transformation (2 Corinthians 5:17) 25

Chapter 10: The Power of Mentorship - A Father Guiding At-Risk Youth (Titus 2:6-8) 27

Chapter 11: Breaking the Cycle of Dysfunction - Practical Solutions (Galatians 6:1-2) 30

Chapter 12: Fatherhood and Family - The Cornerstone of a Thriving Society (Ephesians 6:4) 32

Chapter 13: Overcoming Generational Curses - The Path of Wholeness (Exodus 20:5-6) 35

Chapter 14: A Cry for the Future - Urgent Call for Change 38

Chapter 15: Nurturing the Future Generation - Empowering Our Youth with Wisdom and Guidance (Deuteronomy 6:6-7) 40

Chapter 16: Restoring the Prodigal - Lessons from the Book of Hosea (Hosea 14:1-4) 42

Chapter 17: Incarnation to Transformation - Redemptive Stories (1 Timothy 1:15-16) 44

Chapter 18: The Redemptive Power of Mentorship and Community 47

Chapter 19: Reconciling Families - The Healing Power of Forgiveness (Colossians 3:13) 51

Chapter 20: A Father's Heartfelt Confession 53

Chapter 21: A Father's Unspoken Words 56

Chapter 22: The Role of the Church: Embracing Prodigal Families - Unity in Diversity (Luke 15:20) 58

Chapter 23: Community Transformation - Empowering Fathers and Homes (Isaiah 58:12) 60

Chapter 24: Fulfilling the Prophecy - A Vision for Restoration (Hosea 4;6) 62

Samuel Ben Israel's Story 66

Jacoby Ben Israel's Bio 68

Hezekiah Ben Israel's Story 71

Hezekiah Ben Israel's Bio 73

Author's Note 77

Co-Author's Note 79

These chapter titles and corresponding Scriptures are designed to guide the reader through the journey of restoring families, addressing the root causes of societal challenges, and highlighting the transformative power of faith, mentorship, and redemption.

UNSHACKLED VOICES

Yarah Ben Israel with his Wife

YARAH & SAMUEL BEN ISRAEL

Yarah with daughter & grand daughter

Chapter 1:
Hosea's Prophecy: The Clarion Call (Hosea 4:6)

In the first chapter of our exploration, we delve into the prophetic words of Hosea, as he declared, "My people are destroyed for lack of knowledge" (Hosea 4:6, KJV). This verse serves as a clarion call, a warning to a society adrift in ignorance and apathy. Let us unpack the keywords and delve deeper into their meanings as we apply them to the challenges facing children of incarcerated fathers today.

1. **Destroyed** (Hebrew - shamad): This word denotes destruction, ruin, and devastation. In the context of Hosea's prophecy, it signifies the dire consequences of ignorance and disobedience.

2. **Lack** (Hebrew - chacer): This term conveys a sense of deficiency, insufficiency, and scarcity. It highlights the absence of essential knowledge and understanding.

3. **Knowledge** (Hebrew - da`ath): This word refers to knowledge, wisdom, and discernment. It emphasizes the importance of acquiring and applying wisdom in one's life.

4. **Clarion Call** (Greek - kērygma): This phrase implies a clear, powerful message or proclamation. It serves as a wake-up call, urging individuals to heed the warning and take action.

The dictionary college edition provides additional insights into these terms:

- **Destroyed:** To cause great harm or damage; to be ruined or devastated.

- **Lack:** The state of being without or deficient in something essential.
- **Knowledge:** Information, understanding, or skill acquired through experience or education.
- **Clarion Call:** A clear, emphatic call to action or awareness.

In today's times, children of incarcerated fathers often face significant challenges, including emotional trauma, financial instability, and a lack of positive role models. The prophecy of Hosea resonates with these children, highlighting the destructive impact of ignorance and the deficiency of vital knowledge and support in their lives.

Through mentorship, education, and community outreach programs, we can reach out to these vulnerable youth and provide them with the knowledge and resources they need to thrive. By heeding the clarion call of Hosea's prophecy, we can work towards breaking the cycle of destruction and empowering children of incarcerated fathers to overcome adversity and build a brighter future.

Chapter 2:
The Consequences of Ignorance - Learning from Biblical and Modern-Day Parallels

In Chapter 1, we explored the prophecy of Hosea 4:6, contemplating the profound statement, "My people are destroyed for lack of knowledge" (KJV). Building upon this theme, we continue our exploration into the repercussions of ignorance through the prism of both biblical narratives and contemporary parallels, illuminating the enduring impact of uninformed decisions and actions.

Embarking on a dual narrative journey, we revisit the tragic tale of Adam and Eve in Genesis 3 as a quintessential biblical example of the dire consequences borne of ignorance. Within the idyllic setting of the Garden of Eden, their choice to partake in the forbidden fruit of the Tree of Knowledge of Good and Evil showcases the catastrophic outcomes that arise from a lack of understanding and negligence towards divine directives. Their expulsion from paradise and the introduction of sin into the world serve as poignant reminders of the crucial role that knowledge and obedience play in shaping our destinies.

Shifting to a modern-day parallel, we confront the sobering reality of the opioid crisis, a contemporary scourge fueled by a pervasive lack of awareness and comprehension. Rooted in the ignorance of both prescribers and recipients regarding the addictive nature of opioid medications, this crisis has wrought widespread devastation, claiming lives, fracturing families, and ravaging communities. The profound repercussions of this collective ignorance underscore the critical need for informed decision-making and an unwavering dedication to seeking enlightenment in navigating life's complexities.

By examining these parallel narratives through a comparative lens, we are compelled to recognize the enduring importance of knowledge, wisdom, and discernment in safeguarding against the dangers of ignorance. Just as Adam and Eve's pivotal misstep resonated through the passage of time, so too does the contemporary opioid crisis serve as a testament to the far-reaching consequences of uninformed choices. Through a commitment to seeking understanding, asking probing questions, and aligning our actions with divine purpose, we can transcend the shadows of ignorance and stride confidently in the brilliance of truth and enlightenment.

May the insights gleaned from these past narratives inspire us to cultivate a hunger for knowledge, a spirit of discernment, and a resolve to pursue wisdom across all aspects of our lives. As we navigate the complexities of a world in constant flux, let us shun the pitfalls of ignorance and instead illuminate our paths with the guiding beacon of truth and understanding.

Chapter 3:
The Unraveling of the American Family (Psalms 127:1)

As we turn our attention to the unraveling of the American family, we draw inspiration from Psalms 127:1, which states, "Unless the Lord builds the house, those who build it labor in vain" (ESV). This verse serves as a poignant reminder of the importance of a strong foundation in family life and how without spiritual guidance and support, our efforts may be in vain. Let us dissect the keywords in this verse and explore their implications for children of incarcerated fathers, who often face unique challenges in the absence of a stable family structure.

1. **Builds** (Hebrew - banah): This word conveys the act of constructing or establishing something. In the context of the family, it symbolizes the intentional effort and care required to nurture and maintain a healthy household.

2. **House** (Hebrew - bayit): This term refers to a dwelling place, a household, or a family unit. It represents the physical and emotional space where relationships are formed and nurtured.

3. **Labor** (Hebrew - ya`ats): This word signifies toil, effort, and hard work. It illustrates the diligence and persistence needed to maintain a harmonious family dynamic.

4. **Vain** (Hebrew - reyq): This term denotes emptiness, futility, and failure. It serves as a caution against relying solely on human efforts without seeking divine guidance and wisdom.

The dictionary college edition offers additional insights into these terms:

- **Builds:** To construct or form by assembling parts; to establish or develop.
- **House:** A place of residence or refuge; a familial unit or social group living together.
- **Labor:** Physical or mental exertion; work done with effort and perseverance.
- **Vain:** Lacking substance or worth; producing no result; futile.

Children of incarcerated fathers often bear the brunt of the breakdown in family dynamics, facing emotional, financial, and social challenges as a result. The unraveling of the American family can have a profound impact on these children, leaving them vulnerable and in need of support and guidance.

By recognizing the importance of a strong foundation in family life, we can strive to provide a nurturing and stable environment for children of incarcerated fathers. Through mentorship, counseling, and community outreach programs, we can offer them the love, support, and guidance they need to navigate the complexities of their circumstances and build a brighter future. Just as the psalmist reminds us, it is only with the Lord's guidance and blessing that we can truly build a lasting and meaningful family legacy for future generations.

Continuation

In delving deeper into the unraveling of the American family through the lens of Psalms 127:1, we can spiritualize this concept to understand the timeless wisdom and guidance it offers. Applying the verse to the challenges faced by children of incarcerated fathers, we can draw parallels to the biblical narrative of the Prodigal Son in Luke 15:11-32.

1. **Builds:** Through the story of the Prodigal Son, we see the importance of the Father's unwavering love and guidance in building a strong family foundation. The Father patiently waits for his wayward son, symbolizing the divine guidance and support that children of incarcerated fathers need to navigate their own challenges.

2. **House:** The Father's house in the parable represents a place of refuge and restoration, mirroring the need for a stable and nurturing environment for these children. Just as the father welcomes back his lost son with open arms, so too should we strive to create a supportive and loving atmosphere for those in need.

3. **Labor:** The Father's tireless efforts to reconcile with his son illustrate the perseverance and dedication required to rebuild broken relationships. Through our own labor of love and compassion, we can help guide children of incarcerated fathers toward healing and reconciliation.

4. **Vain:** The Prodigal Son's initial pursuit of worldly pleasures leads to emptiness and despair, highlighting the futility of seeking fulfillment outside of God's loving embrace. By turning to the Son of God for guidance and direction, we can avoid the pitfalls of vanity and find true purpose and meaning in our lives.

As we reflect on the parallels between Psalms 127:1 and the story of the Prodigal Son, let us remember the enduring message of hope and redemption that the Bible offers. By building our families on a foundation of faith, love, and forgiveness, we can overcome the challenges of the present and build a promising future for generations to come. Just as the Father's unwavering love restored the Prodigal Son to his rightful place in the family, so too can we extend God's grace and mercy to those in need of healing and restoration in the American family.

Chapter 4:
The Consequences of Fatherlessness
(Proverbs 22:6)

In Proverbs 22:6, it is written: "Train up a child in the way he should go, and when he is old he will not depart from it."

Let us delve into the meanings of keywords from this verse through the concordance and dictionary, seeking a deeper understanding of the consequences of fatherlessness.

1. **Train** (Hebrew - chanak): This word conveys the act of dedicating, disciplining, and instructing a child. It implies a deliberate effort to shape and guide the development of a young individual.

2. **Child** (Hebrew - na`ar): This term refers to a youth, a servant, or a young person. It symbolizes a stage of growth and vulnerability in which guidance and direction are crucial.

3. **Way** (Hebrew - derek): This word signifies a path, a course of action, or a way of life. It represents the journey that a child embarks upon, guided by the teachings and values instilled by their father figure.

4. **Depart** (Hebrew - sur): This term connotes to turn aside, to go away from, or to abandon. It reflects the potential consequences of neglecting or lacking proper fatherly guidance in a child's life.

The dictionary college edition offers further insights into these terms:

- **Train:** To teach or instruct; to prepare someone for a specific task or role through practice and instruction.

- **Child:** A young human being, a son or daughter; a person in the early stage of life characterized by immaturity and dependency.
- **Way:** A method, manner, or course of action; a direction or path to follow; a habitual practice or behavior.
- **Depart:** To leave or go away from a place or situation; to deviate or stray from a set course or path; to forsake.

The consequences of fatherlessness, as outlined in Proverbs 22:6, serve as a cautionary tale of the importance of parental guidance and support in a child's life. Just as Yahweh, our Heavenly Father, guides us with wisdom and love, so too should earthly fathers provide nurturing and righteous instruction to their children.

Through understanding the significance of fatherhood in shaping the lives of the next generation, we are called to uphold the responsibility of training and guiding our youth, instilling values and principles that will lead them on the path of righteousness. Let us heed the teachings of Proverbs and seek Yahweh's guidance as we strive to fulfill our roles as mentors and fathers, ensuring that our children do not depart from the way they should go.

The absence of fathers from the home can have a significant impact on families, communities, and society as a whole. Fathers play a crucial role in the upbringing and development of their children, providing support, guidance, and love that are essential for their well-being. When fathers are not present in the home, children may lack positive male role models, leading to potential behavioral and emotional issues.

Research has shown that children raised in father-absent homes are more likely to experience a range of negative outcomes, including lower academic achievement, higher rates of substance abuse, delinquency, and criminal behavior. Furthermore, the absence of fathers can contribute to poverty, as single-parent households, often led by mothers, may struggle to provide for the financial needs of the family.

In addition to the impact on individual families, the absence of fathers can also have broader societal consequences. Communities with high rates of father absence may experience higher levels of crime, lower educational attainment, and an overall sense of instability. The lack of positive male role models can also contribute to a cycle of fatherlessness, as children growing up without fathers may struggle to understand their own role as fathers in the future.

Addressing the issue of father's absence requires a multifaceted approach, including support for fathers to actively engage in their children's lives, policies that promote family stability, and community interventions that provide resources and support for families in need. By recognizing the importance of fathers in the home and taking steps to support responsible fatherhood, we can help build stronger families, communities, and, ultimately, a stronger country.

Chapter 5:
Restoring the Foundations: A Biblical Mandate (Psalms 11:3)

In this pivotal chapter, we delve into the profound biblical mandate of restoring the foundations as outlined in Psalms 11:3. This verse serves as a guiding light, reminding us of the importance of preserving and strengthening the core principles that underpin our beliefs and values.

To begin our exploration, let us first dissect the keywords within this verse using a concordance to unlock deeper meanings and insights. By understanding the detonation of each word, we can grasp the full significance of the message conveyed.

1. **Restoring:** This word implies the act of returning something to its original state or condition. It signifies a process of renewal and rejuvenation, highlighting the need to repair and reinforce what may have been damaged or weakened over time.

2. **Foundations:** The foundations represent the fundamental principles or beliefs upon which something is built. They provide stability, support, and structure, forming the bedrock of our faith and existence. Protecting and restoring these foundations is crucial for maintaining resilience and integrity.

3. **Biblical:** This adjective emphasizes the divine inspiration and authority of the Scriptures. The term "biblical" underscores the spiritual significance and timeless wisdom inherent in the Word of God, serving as a beacon of truth and guidance for believers.

4. **Mandate:** A mandate is a directive or command that carries moral or legal authority. In this context, the biblical mandate refers to a solemn obligation or duty prescribed by God, compelling us to uphold and uphold the principles of faith and righteousness.

As we unravel the layers of meaning embedded in Psalms 11:3, we are called to reflect on the profound implications of restoring the foundations of our lives, communities, and societies. The challenges of modern times demand a steadfast commitment to preserving the core values and truths that define our identity and purpose.

In the current landscape of uncertainty and turmoil, the urgency of this biblical mandate cannot be understated. We stand at a critical juncture, poised to embark on a journey of renewal and transformation. As we venture into this time of upheaval and change, let us heed the call to action with seriousness and resolve.

May this chapter serve as a catalyst for introspection, growth, and revival as we strive to uphold the sacred duty of restoring the foundations laid before us. Let us embrace the profound significance of this mandate as we navigate the challenges and opportunities that lie ahead.

You make a powerful and impassioned plea to address the pressing issue of father's absence within our communities. It is a call that resonates deeply for the well-being of families, neighborhoods, and our nation, as a whole, hinges upon the restoration of this vital role.

As you so eloquently articulate, the absence of fathers from the home can have devastating consequences, leading to a cascade of social ills that undermine the fabric of our society. Children deprived of a father's love, guidance, and positive influence are more vulnerable to a host of challenges – from academic struggles to behavioral problems and even criminal activity. The ripple effect of this deprivation is felt throughout the community, eroding the foundation upon which strong, thriving neighborhoods are built.

Yet, within this complex and often overwhelming landscape, there is a glimmer of hope – a ray of light that shines through the darkness. As you so perceptively observe, there are indeed those who have gone through the crucible of incarceration and emerged transformed, their hearts and minds now firmly grounded in the principles of righteousness and service. These individuals, imbued with a deep love for the Almighty and a profound commitment to mentoring others, possess the very qualities that are essential for rebuilding and strengthening families.

It is these men – the ones who have experienced the depths of brokenness and have found the path to restoration – who hold the key to the redemption of our communities. Their testimonies of transformation, their unwavering dedication to their faith, and their innate leadership skills can serve as a powerful beacon, inspiring others to follow in their footsteps and reclaim their roles as fathers, brothers, and pillars of the community.

It is our collective responsibility to ensure that these individuals, having shown themselves ready to return and contribute, are given the opportunity to do so. Through programs and initiatives that facilitate their reintegration, provide them with the necessary support and resources, and empower them to share their stories and wisdom, we can begin to mend the torn fabric of our families and communities.

By embracing the redemptive power of these changed lives, we can bear witness to the profound impact of resilience, faith, and the unwavering belief in the human capacity for growth and restoration. In doing so, we not only honor the sanctity of the family unit but also ignite a spark of hope that can spread far and wide, transforming the landscape of our nation and inspiring a new generation to rise up and lead the way toward a brighter, more unified future.

Chapter 6:
The Testimony of Joseph: Forgiveness and Reconciliation (Genesis 37-50)

In this transformative chapter, we delve into the powerful testimony of Joseph as a symbol of forgiveness and reconciliation, as depicted in the Book of Genesis chapters 37 to 50. Through the lens of Joseph's journey, we unravel the profound lessons of grace, redemption, and divine providence that continue to resonate through the ages.

Let us embark on a journey of exploration by dissecting the keywords present in this remarkable narrative, drawing insights from the concordance and the dictionary to illuminate their meanings and implications. As we delve deeper into Joseph's story, we will weave in the presence of Yahweh, the Almighty God who orchestrates each event for a greater purpose.

1. **Testimony:** The testimony of Joseph signifies a declaration or demonstration of faith, resilience, and virtue in the face of adversity. It serves as a testament to the unwavering trust in Yahweh's plan and providence, inspiring others to walk in righteousness and forgiveness.

2. **Forgiveness:** Forgiveness embodies the act of pardoning or releasing oneself from resentment, anger, or bitterness towards others. Joseph's choice to forgive his brothers for their betrayal exemplifies the transformative power of mercy and reconciliation, guided by the divine grace of Yahweh.

3. **Reconciliation:** Reconciliation denotes the restoration of relationships or harmony between individuals who have been estranged or divided. Through Joseph's reconciliation

with his brothers and his compassionate actions, we witness the healing power of forgiveness and the hand of Yahweh guiding the path toward unity and peace.

4. **Yahweh:** Throughout Joseph's journey, we see the hand of Yahweh at work, orchestrating events and opportunities for redemption and restoration. Yahweh's divine presence is evident in every circumstance, shaping Joseph's path toward fulfillment of the grand plan set forth by the Almighty.

As we reflect on the testimony of Joseph, we are reminded of the enduring values of forgiveness, reconciliation, and unwavering faith in Yahweh's divine providence. Joseph's story serves as a beacon of hope and inspiration, calling us to emulate his example of grace and compassion in the face of adversity.

In a world marked by turmoil and division, the legacy of Joseph resonates as a timeless reminder of the transformative power of forgiveness and reconciliation. Let us heed the call to emulate Joseph's unwavering trust in Yahweh's plan and walk in the path of righteousness and love, fostering unity and harmony in our relationships and communities.

The powerful message you have conveyed, drawing upon the profound insights and wisdom found in the scriptures, resonates deeply in our present-day context. Let us explore how the principles and teachings espoused in these verses can be applied to the pressing challenges we face in our communities and society as a whole.

Verse 5 emphasizes the critical importance of honoring and upholding the role of the father within the family unit. It reminds us that the absence of a father's presence can have far-reaching consequences, not only for the individual child but for the entire community. In our modern era, where the traditional family structure has faced increasing strains and disruptions, this verse serves as a clarion call to prioritize the restoration of the father's rightful place in the home.

By heeding this call, we can begin to address the root causes of many social ills that plague our communities. As you so eloquently stated, the lack of positive male role models can contribute to a cycle of fatherlessness, perpetuating a culture of instability, disconnection, and even criminal behavior. However, by empowering and supporting fathers to actively engage in their children's lives, we can break this cycle and pave the way for healthier, more resilient families.

This is not merely a theoretical construct but a practical imperative that we must collectively embrace. Through initiatives that provide resources, counseling, and mentorship opportunities for fathers, we can equip them with the tools and skills necessary to fulfill their vital role. By fostering an environment that values and uplifts the father's presence, we can inspire more men to step up, take responsibility, and become the pillars of strength and guidance their families and communities desperately need.

Alongside this focus on strengthening the father's role, we must also recognize the transformative power of those who have undergone their own personal journeys of redemption and growth. As you so insightfully observed, there are individuals within our communities who have emerged from the depths of brokenness, their lives now anchored in righteousness, faith, and a deep commitment to mentoring others.

These individuals, having experienced the transformative power of repentance and restoration, possess a unique ability to reach and inspire those who may be struggling with similar challenges. By providing them with platforms to share their stories, impart their wisdom, and serve as living examples of the triumph of the human spirit, we can kindle a spark of hope that can ignite a movement of positive change.

In doing so, we not only uplift the individual lives of those in need but also strengthen the fabric of our communities. As these transformed individuals step forward as leaders, mentors, and role models, they can help guide others toward a path of redemption, fostering an environment of accountability, support, and a renewed commitment to family and community values.

The principles and lessons contained within these verses are not mere historical relics; they are timeless truths that hold the power to transform our present-day reality. By heeding their call to restore the father's role, empower the redeemed, and build a foundation of strong, resilient families, we can chart a course toward a future where our communities and our nation thrive, united in a shared vision of justice, compassion, and the unwavering belief in the human capacity for change.

Yarah with Family

Chapter 7:
The Parable of the Prodigal Son: Redemption (Luke 15:11-32)

In a small town, the story of a father and son mirrored the powerful parable found in Luke 15:11-32. Matthew, a successful businessman and devoted follower of Yahweh, had poured his heart and soul into building a thriving company driven by a desire to provide a comfortable life for his family. Yet, his only son, Ethan, had always felt stifled by his father's high expectations and the confines of their traditional way of life.

As Ethan grew older, his longing for independence and adventure grew stronger. One day, he approached his father and demanded his share of the family inheritance, determined to forge his own path in the world. Matthew, though saddened by his son's decision, knew he could not hold him back. Reluctantly, he fulfilled Ethan's request, watching as the young man set off, chasing his dreams.

At first, Ethan reveled in his newfound freedom, indulging in a lavish and carefree lifestyle. He traveled to distant lands, spending his inheritance on extravagant pleasures, until one day, he found himself penniless and alone, far from the comforts of home. It was then that the weight of his choices hit him, and he realized the folly of his ways.

Humbled and penitent, Ethan made the difficult decision to return to his father's house, prepared to plead for forgiveness and accept any consequences that may come. As he approached the familiar estate, his heart raced, unsure of the reception he would receive.

But to Ethan's surprise, the moment his father, Matthew, caught sight of him, the older man's face broke into a joyous smile. Without hesitation, Matthew ran to embrace his long-lost son, his eyes shining with tears of relief and unconditional love. In that moment, Ethan felt the weight of his guilt and shame lift, as his father welcomed him back with open arms.

Matthew quickly ordered the best robe to be placed on Ethan's shoulders, a ring on his finger, and a grand feast to be prepared – symbols of the restoration and reconciliation that had taken place. The Father's extravagant display of forgiveness and acceptance mirrored the boundless grace that the Son of Yahweh extends to all who repent and seek to be reconciled with the Heavenly Father.

This story of the prodigal son's homecoming serves as a powerful testament to the transformative power of repentance and the enduring love of a father. It reminds us that no matter how far we may stray, the embrace of Yahweh and His Son is always waiting to welcome us back, ready to restore broken relationships and heal wounded hearts.

For fathers and sons who find themselves in similar struggles, this parable offers a message of hope and reconciliation. It encourages fathers to let go of their own expectations and meet their children with compassion while guiding sons to recognize the value of their father's wisdom and the security of a loving home. Through forgiveness and grace, the wounds of the past can be healed, and the bond between father and son can be strengthened, reflecting the unconditional love and restoration offered by Yahweh and His Son.

Chapter 8:
The Parable of the Prodigal Son: Restoration (Luke 15:11-32)

In a modern setting, the parable of the Prodigal Son takes on a fresh relevance, reflecting the reconciliation between a father and his estranged son during the father's incarnation.

1. Prodigal (G811 - "to consume, spend, waste extravagantly") - A young man named Ethan, the son of a successful businessman named Matthew, had long struggled with the constraints of his father's traditional values and expectations. Ethan's desire for independence and "prodigal" (G811) living led him to demand his "portion" (G3313) of the family inheritance.

2. Ponder (G1256 - "to think about carefully, consider") - With his newfound freedom, Ethan "pondered" (G1256) little as he "indulged" (G1159) in a lavish lifestyle, eventually squandering his resources and finding himself "destitute" (G3993) and "desperate" (G5302). It was in this moment of desperation that Ethan "realized" (G1097) the "folly" (G454) of his choices and the unconditional love he had taken for granted.

3. Pacify (G4160 - "to do, make, produce, act") - Humbled and "penitent" (G3340), Ethan "decided" (G1014) to return to his father's home, "prepared" (G2090) to "plead" (G2065) for "forgiveness" (G859) and "accept" (G1209) any "consequences" (G2920) of his actions.

4. Provide (G4016 - "to furnish, supply, provide") - To Ethan's surprise, when he "approached" (G1448) the family estate,

his father, Matthew, "saw" (G3708) him from a distance and "ran" (G5143) to "embrace" (G4843) his long-lost son. Matthew "rejoiced" (G5463) at Ethan's return, "providing" (G4016) him with the best robe, a ring, and a celebratory feast, symbolizing the "unconditional" (G571) love and "forgiveness" (G859) that the Son of Yahweh extends to all who repent and seek to be "reconciled" (G2433).

In this modern retelling, the parable's themes of grace, forgiveness, and the restoration of relationships take on a deeper significance. The incarnation of Matthew, the father, represents the Son of Yahweh's own incarnation, who came to earth to reconcile humanity with the Heavenly Father.

Just as the prodigal son was welcomed back with open arms, the Son of Yahweh's love and forgiveness is extended to all who turn away from their prodigal ways and seek to be restored in their relationship with Yahweh. This powerful narrative serves as a testament to the transformative power of repentance and the boundless grace that Yahweh offers to those who are willing to come home.

Chapter 9:
From Darkness to Light - An Incarcerated Father's Transformation (2 Corinthians 5:17)

In the United States, the struggle of incarcerated fathers to reconnect with their children is a heartbreaking reality. Statistics reveal the sobering truth: according to the Bureau of Justice, in 2019, nearly 58% of state and 63% of federal prisoners were parents of minor children. Tragically, many of these fathers never even have the chance to visit their children, with a staggering 49% of state and 55% of federal prisoners reporting that they have never had a personal visit from their child.

The story of Matthew and Ethan, however, offers a glimmer of hope in the midst of this darkness. Matthew, a once-successful businessman, had found himself incarcerated for a financial crime, leaving his son Ethan to navigate the challenges of growing up without a present father.

During his time in prison, Matthew was confronted with the harsh realities of his choices and the profound impact they had on his family. He wrestled with feelings of guilt, shame, and a deep longing to make amends. It was then that he encountered the transformative power of the gospel, as he discovered the redeeming love and grace of Yahweh and His Son.

Through the support of a prison ministry and the constant encouragement of a fellow inmate who had also experienced a spiritual awakening, Matthew began to undergo a profound transformation. He committed himself to prayer, Bible study, and personal reflection, seeking to find the path back to his son and the restoration of their broken relationship.

As Matthew's heart softened and his mindset shifted, he began to take concrete steps toward reconciliation. He wrote heartfelt letters to Ethan, expressing his remorse and his unwavering love. Slowly, the barriers of bitterness and resentment began to crumble, and Ethan, though initially skeptical, could sense the sincerity of his father's repentance.

When Matthew's sentence was finally completed, he returned home with a renewed sense of purpose and a deep desire to rebuild the bridges he had burned. He approached Ethan, humbly asking for forgiveness and the opportunity to rebuild their relationship. Ethan, touched by the genuine change he witnessed in his father, was moved to extend grace and embark on the journey of reconciliation.

Together, they embarked on a path of healing, guided by the principles of 2 Corinthians 5:17, which declares, "Therefore, if anyone is in Christ, the new creation has come: The old has gone, the new is here!" Matthew's transformation from a careless, incarcerated father to a renewed, committed parent served as a powerful testimony to the transformative power of Yahweh's love and the redemptive work of His Son.

This story is not an isolated incident but rather a reflection of the many fathers who have found the courage to turn their lives around and reclaim their roles as loving, present parents. By embracing the light of Yahweh's grace and the wisdom found in His Word, these men have been able to confront their past mistakes, seek forgiveness, and rebuild meaningful relationships with their children.

The journey from darkness to light is never an easy one, but it is a path that holds the promise of redemption and restoration. As more fathers like Matthew take the courageous step to surrender their lives to Yahweh and the son, the cycle of broken families can be transformed, bringing hope and healing to generations to come.

Chapter 10:
The Power of Mentorship - A Father Guiding At-Risk Youth (Titus 2:6-8)

In the book of Titus, the Apostle Paul provides clear guidance on the importance of mentorship, particularly for young men. In Titus 2:6-8, he exhorts: "Similarly, encourage the young men to be self-controlled. In everything, set them an example by doing what is good. In your teaching, show integrity, seriousness, and soundness of speech that cannot be condemned so that those who oppose you may be ashamed because they have nothing bad to say about us."

This passage underscores the vital role that older, wiser men have in shaping the lives of the younger generation. As the world grows increasingly complex and the challenges facing youth more daunting, the need for strong, positive male mentors has never been greater.

This is precisely the story of Michael, a father who understood the transformative power of mentorship. Growing up in an impoverished neighborhood, Michael had witnessed firsthand the devastating effects of absent fathers and the pull of destructive influences on at-risk youth. Determined to break the cycle, he committed himself to becoming a beacon of hope and guidance for the young men in his community.

Guided by the principles of Yahweh's Word and the example set by the Son of Yahweh, Michael opened his home and his heart to young men who were struggling to find their way. He invited them to join him in Bible study, engaging them in discussions about the importance of self-control, integrity, and righteous living. Through his own actions, he demonstrated what it meant to be a man of Yahweh, setting an example of moral fortitude and unwavering faith.

As these young men spent time with Michael, they began to see their own lives through a new lens. They witnessed the power of a father's guidance and the transformative impact of a positive male role model. Slowly but surely, they started to shed the destructive behaviors and negative mindsets that had once defined them, embracing a path of personal growth and spiritual renewal.

The ripple effects of Michael's mentorship were profound. Several of the young men he had taken under his wing went on to become leaders in their communities, using their own stories of redemption to inspire and guide others. One young man, whose own father had been incarcerated, became a youth pastor, pouring into the lives of at-risk teens, just as Michael had done for him.

The statistics on the impact of fatherly presence in a child's life are staggering. According to the U.S. Census Bureau, children who grow up without a father in the home are four times more likely to live in poverty and twice as likely to drop out of school. Tragically, many of these children never have the opportunity to experience the guidance and support of a male mentor, even after their fathers are released from incarceration.

However, the story of Michael and the young men he mentored stands as a powerful testament to the transformative power of a father's influence. By heeding the call of Titus 2:6-8 and stepping into the lives of those in need, men like Michael can make a profound difference, guiding the next generation to find their purpose, their identity, and their connection to the Heavenly Father and His Son.

Through the provision of stable, loving mentorship, the cycle of brokenness and despair can be broken and replaced by a future of hope, purpose, and lasting transformation. It is a reminder that the power of a father's influence, coupled with the grace and wisdom of

Yahweh's Word, can be the light that leads even the most at-risk youth out of the darkness and into the abundant life that Yahweh and His Son have promised.

Chapter 11:
Breaking the Cycle of Dysfunction - Practical Solutions (Galatians 6:1-2)

In the Epistle to the Galatians, the Apostle Paul offers profound guidance on how to address the complex issues of dysfunction and brokenness within our communities. In Galatians 6:1-2, he writes, "Brothers and sisters, if someone is caught in a sin, you who live by the Spirit should restore that person gently. But watch yourselves, or you also may be tempted. Carry each other's burdens, and in this way, you will fulfill the law of Christ."

This passage provides a blueprint for how we, as a society, can begin to break the cycle of dysfunction that has led to the alarming rates of fatherlessness and incarceration in the United States.

First, we must approach the issue with a spirit of gentleness and compassion, recognizing that those caught in the grip of dysfunction are often victims themselves, struggling beneath the weight of their own burdens. Rather than condemn or ostracize them, we must extend a hand of restoration, guiding them toward healing and redemption.

This starts with acknowledging the foundational role that fathers play in the lives of their children. The data is clear: children who grow up without a present, engaged father are more likely to struggle with a host of social, emotional, and behavioral issues, ultimately increasing their risk of involvement in the criminal justice system.

However, the problem is not simply one of absentee fathers; it is a complex web of societal factors, including poverty, lack of access to resources, generational trauma, and a criminal justice system that often fails to address the root causes of dysfunction.

To break this cycle, we must call upon our government officials to take a hard look at the policies and practices that have contributed to the erosion of the family unit. This means advocating for criminal justice reform, investing in community-based programs that support fathers and families, and shifting the focus from punishment to rehabilitation and restoration.

As the Apostle Paul instructs, we must be willing to "carry each other's burdens" - to come alongside those who are struggling and walk with them on the path towards healing and wholeness. This can take many forms, from mentorship programs that pair at-risk youth with positive male role models to support groups that provide resources and guidance for incarcerated fathers and their families.

Ultimately, the solution lies in a holistic, compassionate approach that recognizes the inherent dignity and potential of every individual. By addressing the systemic issues that have led to the breakdown of the family and by offering a helping hand to those caught in the cycle of dysfunction, we can begin to restore the "land flowing with milk and honey" - a society where fathers and sons are reunited, and the promises of Yahweh and His Son are realized in the lives of all His children.

This will not be an easy task, and it will require a concerted effort from all corners of our society. But if we approach it with the spirit of gentleness and grace that the Apostle Paul advocates, we can begin to tear down the blindfolds that have obscured the true face of justice, allowing us to see ourselves in the struggles of those we have too often condemned.

It is time to break the cycle of dysfunction, to reclaim the sacred role of fatherhood, and to usher in a new era of restoration and redemption. By working together, guided by the wisdom of Yahweh's Word and the example of His Son, we can create a future where every child, regardless of their circumstances, can thrive and fulfill the purpose that Yahweh has ordained for them.

Chapter 12:
Fatherhood and Family - The Cornerstone of a Thriving Society (Ephesians 6:4)

In the Epistle to the Ephesians, the Apostle Paul provides clear guidance on the vital role of fathers in shaping the lives of their children. He writes, "Fathers, do not exasperate your children; instead, bring them up in the training and instruction of the Lord" (Ephesians 6:4). This passage underscores the profound responsibility that fathers have in nurturing the next generation, just as Yahweh the Father and the Son of Yahweh have done for us.

My fellow Americans, it is time for us to recognize that the foundation of a thriving society lies in the strength and stability of our families. The role of the father, as the cornerstone of the family unit, is essential in providing the spiritual, emotional, and practical support that our children so desperately need.

Yet, as we look around our nation, we see a troubling trend – the erosion of the family, the breakdown of the father-child relationship, and the devastating consequences that have followed. Too many of our children are growing up without the guidance and support of a present, engaged father, leaving them vulnerable to the pull of destructive influences and the despair of a life without purpose.

The statistics are sobering: children raised in single-parent households are more likely to experience poverty, struggle academically, and become involved in the criminal justice system. The absence of a father's influence has a profound and lasting impact on the lives of our young people, shaping their identities, their values, and their very futures.

But this is not a problem that we can simply ignore or dismiss. As a people, as a nation, we must come together and acknowledge the urgent need to repair the crumbling foundations of our families. We must recognize that a society with missing or damaged cornerstones – the fathers who are meant to be the pillars of strength and stability – is more susceptible to collapse.

It is time to take action, to invest in programs and initiatives that support fathers and strengthen the family unit. This means providing access to resources, counseling, and mentorship opportunities that empower fathers to be the leaders, protectors, and nurturers that their children need. It means advocating for policies and legislation that address the systemic issues that have contributed to the erosion of the family, such as poverty, job insecurity, and the failings of our criminal justice system.

But more than that, it means a shift in our collective mindset – a recognition that the restoration of fatherhood is not just a personal or familial issue but a societal imperative. We must come to see the father's role as the cornerstone of a thriving society, a foundation upon which our children can build lives of purpose, meaning, and lasting impact.

Just as Yahweh the Father and the Son of Yahweh have provided the unshakable foundation for our spiritual lives, so too must we, as a people, commit ourselves to the task of rebuilding the family unit, one father at a time. It is a daunting challenge, to be sure, but it is one that we must embrace if we are to secure a brighter future for our nation and our world.

My fellow Americans, the time for action is now. Let us come together, guided by the wisdom of Yahweh's Word and the example of the Son, to repair the cracks in the cornerstones of our families and communities. For in doing so, we will not only restore the strength and stability of our society, but we will also fulfill the sacred calling to nurture and guide the next generation – to raise up a people who will carry on the legacy of Yahweh's love and the Son's redemption.

Chapter 13:
Overcoming Generational Curses - The Path of Wholeness (Exodus 20:5-6)

In a small, rundown neighborhood on the outskirts of a bustling city, there lived a family named the Thompsons. For generations, the Thompsons had been known for their troubled past – a lineage marked by crime, incarceration, and at-risk teen children. They were the outcasts of the community, shunned and rejected by those around them who saw them only as troublemakers and lost causes.

The curse seemed to hang over the Thompson family like a dark cloud, following them wherever they went. The father, John Thompson, had been in and out of prison for most of his adult life, leaving his wife, Sarah, to care for their three children on her own. The kids, Tony, Maya, and David, grew up in a world of poverty, violence, and despair, with few opportunities for a better future.

The community turned a blind eye to the Thompsons, refusing to offer any help or support. They were seen as a lost cause, a family destined to repeat the mistakes of their ancestors. Even the government seemed to have given up on them, providing little more than meager assistance that kept them trapped in a cycle of poverty and hopelessness.

But amidst the darkness, there was a glimmer of hope. A small group of individuals, guided by a sense of compassion and a belief in second chances, reached out to the Thompson family. They offered support, mentorship, and a vision for a promising future – one that was full of possibility and potential.

As the Thompsons began to receive the help they so desperately needed, a transformation began to take place. John, the father, found a new purpose and direction in his life, determined to break free from the cycle of incarceration that had plagued his family for generations. Sarah, the mother, discovered inner strength and resilience she never knew she had, providing a stable and loving home for her children.

Tony, Maya, and David, the at-risk teens, were given the opportunity to pursue their dreams and aspirations, breaking free from the limitations that had been placed upon them by their family history. They were encouraged to believe in themselves, to strive for excellence, and to forge a new path for future generations.

As the Thompson family worked together to overcome the generational curse that had held them captive for so long, they found solace and strength in the words of Yahweh from Exodus 20:5-6. He promised to show love to a thousand generations of those who love Him and keep His commandments but also warned of the consequences of sin being passed down to future generations.

Yahweh's words served as a reminder that the path to wholeness and healing lay in turning away from the patterns of the past and embracing a new way of living. The Thompsons realized that they had the power to break free from the chains of their past and create a new legacy for themselves and their descendants.

In conclusion, to overcome the curse of the giant that had plagued the Thompson family and many others like them, three powerful solutions were needed:

1. **Education and Empowerment:** Providing access to quality education, job training, and mentorship programs that equip individuals with the skills and resources needed to break free from the cycle of poverty and incarceration.

2. **Changing Policies and Practices:** Advocating for criminal justice reform, including an examination of unfair sentencing

enhancements that disproportionately impact fatherless homes and perpetuate the cycle of dysfunction.

3. **Community Support and Compassion:** Building a community that offers love, support, and acceptance to those who are struggling, recognizing that everyone deserves a second chance and the opportunity to create a better future for themselves and their families.

By embracing these solutions and working together to address the root causes of generational curses, we can pave the way for a future where families like the Thompsons are not defined by their past, but by the strength, resilience, and potential that lies within them. Let us heed the words of Yahweh and walk the path of wholeness, breaking free from the chains that bind us and stepping into a brighter and more hopeful tomorrow.

Chapter 14:
A Cry for the Future - Urgent Call for Change

As I sit here, feeling the weight of the world on my shoulders, I can't help but think of the children. Our children, the future of our nation, are depending on us. They are looking to us for guidance, for support, for love. But are we giving them what they truly need to thrive, to succeed, to shine bright in a world that can often feel so dark?

I look around and I see the struggles, the challenges, the pain that so many of our youth are facing. They are lost in a sea of uncertainty, craving stability, direction, and hope. They are crying out for help, for someone to show them the way, to believe in them, to invest in their future.

We, as parents, as mentors, as leaders, hold the key to unlocking their potential, to nurturing their souls, to shaping their destinies. It starts with us, right here, right now. We must be the ones to step up, to take action, to make a difference in their lives.

I acknowledge my own faults, my own mistakes, and my own shortcomings. I have failed at times, lost my way, stumbled in the darkness. But I refuse to let that define me, define us. We have the power within us to change the course of history, to rewrite the narrative, and to build a better world for our children.

In Deuteronomy 6:6-7, the text emphasizes the importance of teaching and instructing the next generation about the commandments of the Lord. This instruction serves as a defense against the challenges and distractions present in today's fast-paced world. By instilling these teachings in our children and ensuring they are always on their minds and hearts, we equip them to navigate the complexities of modern life with a strong foundation rooted in faith and understanding.

This is a plea, a cry from the depths of my soul, begging for a revolution of love, of compassion, of empowerment. Our youth need us more than ever. They need us to see them, to hear them, to lift them up.

Let us not wait another moment, another day, another year. The time is now; the urgency is real. We must come together, hand in hand, heart in heart, and pour out our love, our support, our guidance to the next generation. I pray that this message is heard, felt, and embraced by all who have the power to make a difference. Let us rise up, let us stand tall, and let us nurture our children with all the love and care they deserve. Our future depends on it.

Chapter 15:
Nurturing the Future Generation - Empowering Our Youth with Wisdom and Guidance (Deuteronomy 6:6-7)

In a world filled with turmoil and uncertainty, it is essential that we, as parents, mentors, and leaders, prioritize the nurturing and development of our children. The foundation of a strong and prosperous society lies in the hands of the next generation, and it is our responsibility to equip them with the tools they need to succeed.

As stated in Deuteronomy 6:6-7, we are instructed to teach our children diligently, to speak of the commandments of the Lord when we sit at home, when we walk along the road, when we lie down, and when we rise up. This passage serves as a reminder of the importance of instilling values, beliefs, and morals in our youth, ensuring that they are well-equipped to navigate the complexities of the world with grace and wisdom.

As parents, it is crucial that we lead by example, showing our children what it means to live a life of integrity, compassion, and purpose. We must be active participants in their lives, offering guidance, support, and love every step of the way. By creating a nurturing and supportive environment at home, we lay the groundwork for our children to grow into responsible, compassionate, and empathetic individuals.

But it is not just the responsibility of parents to nurture the next generation. Mentors, teachers, and community leaders all play a vital role in shaping the lives of our youth. By offering guidance, support, and opportunities for growth, we can empower our children to reach their full potential and become productive members of society.

In order to reach the youth effectively, we must offer them early exposure to positive role models, educational opportunities, and real-world experiences. By providing mentorship programs, educational resources, and career guidance, we can help our youth discover their passions, develop essential skills, and pursue their dreams with confidence.

As we look to the future, it is crucial that we prepare our youth for leadership roles in society. Just as Yahweh instructs us to be prepared, we must equip our children with the knowledge, skills, and values they need to lead with compassion, integrity, and vision. By investing in their education, nurturing their talents, and fostering their growth, we can ensure that the upcoming generation is prepared to take on the challenges of tomorrow with resilience and grace.

It is only through collective effort, dedication, and love that we can truly nurture the next generation and build a better world for all. Let us stand united in our commitment to empowering our youth, shaping their destinies, and ensuring a brighter future for generations to come.

Chapter 16:
Restoring the Prodigal - Lessons from the Book of Hosea (Hosea 14:1-4)

In the book of Hosea, we are presented with a powerful narrative of redemption, grace, and restoration by Yahweh. The prophet Hosea, guided by the hand of Yahweh, delivers a message of love and forgiveness to the people of Israel, calling them to return to Yahweh and seek reconciliation for their transgressions. Through the story of Hosea and his unfaithful wife, Gomer, we see a reflection of Yahweh's unwavering love for His people despite their waywardness and sin.

Hosea 14:1-4 captures the essence of this message, as the prophet implores the people to return to Yahweh, to acknowledge their sins, and to seek His forgiveness. The passage speaks of turning away from idols and false gods and instead coming before Yahweh with words of repentance and contrition. Hosea urges the people to recognize their need for Yahweh's mercy and grace and to trust in His promises of restoration and healing.

As we reflect on the lessons from the book of Hosea and the theme of restoring the prodigal, we are reminded of the timeless truths found in the Bible. The story of the prodigal son in the Gospel of Luke serves as a powerful illustration of redemption and forgiveness, as the wayward son returns to his father, humbled and repentant, and is welcomed with open arms and lavish grace.

In the same way, we are called to emulate the love and forgiveness shown by Yahweh towards His people. We are reminded of the need to extend grace and compassion to those who have strayed from the path, offer a hand of reconciliation and restoration, and embody the qualities of forgiveness and mercy that are central to the teachings of Jesus Christ.

The concept of restoring the prodigal is not limited to individuals; it applies to communities, nations, and societies as well. Just as the people of Israel were called to repentance and renewal, so too are we called to examine our collective conscience, acknowledge our failings, and seek reconciliation and healing in our relationships with one another.

As we approach the conclusion of this book, let us remember the profound lessons of grace and restoration found in the book of Hosea. Let us strive to embody the qualities of love, forgiveness, and reconciliation in all aspects of our lives, and to work towards the restoration of the prodigal within ourselves and our world. May we walk in the footsteps of Yahweh's unfailing love and mercy, seeking to bring about redemption and healing wherever we go.

Chapter 17:
Incarnation to Transformation - Redemptive Stories (1 Timothy 1:15-16)

In the quiet corners of a prison cell, where the relentless sounds of chains and despair echo through the darkness, there lies a father. A father who once walked a path veiled in shadows, who bore the weight of his mistakes and the burden of his sins. Yet, in the depths of his solitude, he found solace in the presence of Yahweh, the ever-faithful One who never forsakes His children.

This father, with tears streaming down his face, cries out to Yahweh, longing to be reunited with his beloved family. His heart aches with the absence of laughter and joy that once filled his home, now replaced by the harsh silence of separation. But in his brokenness, he finds strength in the promise of redemption and restoration that Yahweh offers to those who turn to Him in repentance.

Through the bars of his confinement, this father embraces a journey of transformation, guided by the grace and mercy of Yahweh. He commits himself to becoming a better father, to shedding the cloak of his past transgressions and embracing a new identity rooted in love and compassion. With every step he takes towards healing, Yahweh stands beside him, rejoicing in the redemption that unfolds before His eyes.

And with a voice filled with conviction and love, the father raises his eyes to the heavens and offers a spoken prayer to Yahweh for his child:

"O Yahweh, mighty and merciful, hear my plea. Though I am bound by chains of my own making, let my prayers for my child reach you, O Lord. Protect them, guide them, and surround them with Your everlasting love. May they feel Your presence in the absence of my own, and may they know that I lift them up to You in faith and trust. Grant them strength in times of weakness, comfort in times of sorrow, and wisdom in times of confusion. I surrender my child into Your hands, knowing that Your will is perfect and Your love is unfailing. Amen."

In the stillness of the prison gates, where the cries of the forgotten reverberate through the halls, this father's voice resounds with hope and faith. His story, once unheard, now echoes with the redemptive power of Yahweh's love, transforming his life from despair to deliverance, from bondage to freedom.

As we reflect on the redemptive stories of these fathers, let us be reminded of Yahweh's unending capacity for forgiveness and transformation. Let us be inspired by the resilience and faith of those who seek redemption in the face of adversity, and let us stand together in prayer, lifting up the voices of the unheard and the marginalized, knowing that Yahweh's grace is sufficient for all who call upon His name.

It's truly inspiring to hear about the impact of programs like the Jack Brewer Hero's Foundation in mentoring and equipping fathers behind bars for reentry. The transformation and support provided to these struggling men of Yahweh through such programs are a testament to the redemptive power of faith and community.

The involvement of individuals like Mr. Jack Brewer, who embodies the devotion and compassion of Yahweh, is crucial in helping these fathers find hope and strength in their journey toward reintegration into society. By extending a hand of support and guidance, these mentors not only inspire change but also serve as beacons of light in the darkness of despair.

Your decision to write your first book, inspired by the experiences and transformations witnessed through the program, is a powerful testimony to the impact of mentorship and divine intervention. Through your words, you have the opportunity to share stories of redemption, hope, and resilience, further spreading the message of Yahweh's love and grace.

As you continue on your own journey of healing and transformation, may your book serve as a source of inspiration and encouragement to others facing similar challenges. Through your writing, may you magnify the work of Yahweh in the lives of those who have found solace and renewal through programs like the Jack Brewer Hero's Foundation.

May your book be a beacon of light for those in need of guidance and may it amplify the voices of fathers seeking redemption and restoration. And as you reflect on the impact of mentors like Mr. Jack Brewer, may you continue to be a vessel of Yahweh's love and grace, shining brightly in a world that often feels dark and hopeless.

Chapter 18:
The Redemptive Power of Mentorship and Community

It fills my heart with immense joy and gratitude to witness the profound impact of programs like the Jack Brewer Hero's Foundation in guiding and empowering fathers behind bars for their reentry journey. The transformative experiences and unwavering support provided to these men of Yahweh through such initiatives stand as a powerful testament to the redeeming power of faith and community.

The dedication and compassion displayed by individuals like Mr. Jack Brewer, who embodies the very essence of Yahweh's love and mercy, are instrumental in helping these fathers rediscover hope and resilience on their path to reintegrating into society. As a mentor myself, I am deeply moved by the opportunity to extend a helping hand and offer guidance to those in need, inspiring change and serving as a beacon of light in the midst of darkness and despair.

In the spirit of Malachi's timeless wisdom, which calls for the hearts of fathers to be turned back to their children and the hearts of children back to their fathers, the program teaches invaluable lessons on becoming active and present fathers in our children's lives. The program imparts crucial teachings that include:

1. The importance of communication and active listening in fostering strong parent-child relationships.

2. The significance of leading by example and demonstrating integrity and responsibility.

3. The value of quality time spent together and creating lasting memories with our children.

4. The impact of unconditional love, support, and encouragement in nurturing a child's growth and well-being.

5. The power of forgiveness and reconciliation in building and repairing familial bonds.

The involvement of individuals like Mr. Jack Brewer, who embodies the devotion and compassion of Yahweh, is crucial in helping these fathers find hope and strength in their journey toward reintegration into society. By extending a hand of support and guidance, these mentors not only inspire change but also serve as beacons of light in the darkness of despair.

Your decision to write your first book, inspired by the experiences and transformations witnessed through the program, is a powerful testimony to the impact of mentorship and divine intervention. Through your words, you have the opportunity to share stories of redemption, hope, and resilience, further spreading the message of Yahweh's love and grace.

As you continue on your journey of healing and transformation, may your book serve as a source of inspiration and encouragement to others facing similar challenges. Through your writing, may you magnify the work of Yahweh in the lives of those who have found solace and renewal through programs like the Jack Brewer Hero's Foundation.

May your book be a beacon of light for those in need of guidance and may it amplify the voices of fathers seeking redemption and restoration. And as you reflect on the impact of mentors like Mr. Jack Brewer, may you continue to be a vessel of Yahweh's love and grace, shining brightly in a world that often feels dark and hopeless.

The concept of the "beacon of light" that you have so eloquently described is a powerful metaphor for the transformative potential of those who have found redemption and restoration after periods of brokenness and incarceration. Let us delve deeper into how this beacon can illuminate a path forward for both the formerly incarcerated fathers and the community members who embrace their renewed mindsets.

Imagine a young man, once lost in the cycle of crime and poor decision-making, who has now emerged from the shadows of his past, his heart and mind reawakened to the teachings of righteousness. This individual, having experienced the profound impact of mentorship, guidance, and a profound connection to the divine, now stands as a beacon of hope for others who find themselves on a similar journey.

As this transformed individual steps forward, sharing his story of redemption and the lessons he has learned, he becomes a living embodiment of the power of change. His authenticity, his unwavering commitment to his faith, and his genuine desire to uplift and empower others serve as a clarion call to those who may be struggling with their own demons.

Society can positively engage with these renewed mindsets in several meaningful ways:

1. **Mentorship and Guidance:** Community organizations, faith-based institutions, and government programs can create mentorship initiatives that pair the formerly incarcerated fathers with individuals or groups who can provide guidance, support, and a roadmap for successful reintegration into society. This mutual exchange of wisdom and experience can be transformative for both the mentor and the mentee.

2. **Skills Development and Employment Opportunities:** By investing in vocational training, job placement programs, and entrepreneurial support, society can empower these fathers with the necessary tools and resources to rebuild their lives, provide for their families, and contribute positively to their communities. Removing barriers to employment and

fostering pathways to financial stability can be a powerful catalyst for change.

3. **Family Reunification and Strengthening:** Programs that facilitate the reunification of formerly incarcerated fathers with their children and families while also providing counseling, parenting classes, and family-oriented activities can help heal the wounds of separation and rebuild the foundation of the family unit. This holistic approach addresses the multifaceted needs of these individuals and their loved ones.

4. **Community Involvement and Leadership Development:** Encouraging the participation of these renewed-mindset individuals in community-based initiatives, such as youth outreach programs, neighborhood watch groups, or faith-based organizations, can harness their leadership skills, passion for service, and firsthand experiences to inspire and uplift others who may be facing similar challenges.

As these beacons of light step forward, their stories and actions can ripple through the community, igniting a spirit of hope, resilience, and collective responsibility. By embracing and supporting these transformed individuals, society can foster an environment where redemption is celebrated and the power of the human spirit to overcome adversity is celebrated and amplified.

In doing so, we not only contribute to the healing and restoration of the formerly incarcerated fathers but also strengthen the fabric of our communities, creating a tapestry of interconnected lives bound by a shared commitment to justice, compassion, and the boundless potential of human transformation.

Chapter 19: Reconciling Families - The Healing Power of Forgiveness (Colossians 3:13)

Throughout the journey of exploring the impact of programs like the Jack Brewer Hero's Foundation on incarcerated fathers with children, we have witnessed the transformative power of mentorship, faith, and community in guiding these fathers toward redemption and reintegration. From the struggles faced behind bars to the moments of hope and strength found through support and guidance, each chapter of this story has been a testament to the resilience and potential for positive change within these individuals.

The involvement of mentors like Mr. Jack Brewer, who embodies the compassion and devotion of Yahweh, has played a crucial role in helping these fathers find their way back to their families and communities. By extending a hand of support and leading by example, these mentors have shown these fathers that forgiveness, love, and redemption are within reach.

The program has instilled valuable lessons on communication, responsibility, integrity, and the importance of being present in their children's lives. Through teachings rooted in faith and compassion, these fathers have learned to rebuild relationships, create lasting memories, and embrace the power of forgiveness in healing and reconciling with their families.

As these fathers transition back into society, they carry with them the teachings and support they have received, equipping them to become better fathers, role models, and members of their communities. The redemptive journey they have embarked on serves as a beacon of hope and inspiration for others facing similar challenges, showing that with faith, perseverance, and a supportive community, transformation and healing are possible.

In drawing a conclusion to this narrative of reconciliation and restoration, we are reminded of the powerful words found in Colossians 3:13, "Bear with each other and forgive one another if any of you has a grievance against someone. Forgive as the Lord forgave you." These words encapsulate the essence of the healing power of forgiveness, both for the fathers seeking redemption and for the families and communities ready to embrace them with open arms.

As we reflect on the journeys of these fathers and the impact of programs like the Jack Brewer Hero's Foundation, we are reminded of the transformative potential of faith, mentorship, and community in rebuilding lives and reconciling families. Through forgiveness and love, these fathers have found a path toward healing and renewal, inspiring us all to seek reconciliation in our own lives and communities.

In the end, the story of incarcerated fathers with children is not just one of struggle and redemption but also a testament to the enduring power of forgiveness and the resilience of the human spirit in overcoming adversity. As we continue to support and uplift these fathers in their journey toward reconciliation, may we all be reminded of the healing power of forgiveness and the opportunity for renewal that awaits those who seek it.

Chapter 20:
A Father's Heartfelt Confession

My beloved son, it is with a heavy heart that I write these words to you from behind these prison walls. There has not been a single day that has passed where you were not on my mind, where I did not long to be by your side to witness all your firsts, to share in your joys and sorrows. I have written you countless letters in the hopes of reaching out to you, of bridging the gap that separates us. I understand the pain and anger that must consume you, for my absence has left a void that no words can fill.

I have spent many sleepless nights questioning my choices, asking Yahweh why the Holy Spirit has not intervened to reunite us. I have wept in solitude, my heart aching with the knowledge that I have let you down, that I have failed you in ways that I can never fully comprehend. I have been blinded by these walls, unaware of the battles you may have faced, the triumphs and tribulations that have shaped you into the person you are today.

Son, I want you to know that I am aware of my shortcomings, of the ways in which I have disappointed you. I ask for your forgiveness, not out of entitlement, but out of a genuine desire to make amends, to rebuild the shattered pieces of our relationship. I pray that you can find it in your heart to see beyond my faults, to recognize the love that has always been etched in the depths of my soul for you.

As I pen these words, tears stream down my face, for I have missed out on so much, on the chance to be a guiding light in your life. Did you doubt my love for you? Did you question whether I cared? Please know that every beat of my heart has carried your name, that every breath I take is laden with the hope of one day holding you close once more.

I am not perfect, my son, but I am willing to learn, grow, and be the father you deserve. Let us embark on this journey together, let us break down these barriers and forge a new bond that is rooted in understanding, compassion, and unconditional love. May these words find their way to your wounded heart, may they serve as a testament to the undying devotion that resides within me for you, my precious child.

With all my love and remorse,

Your father

Yarah with Family

Chapter 21:
A Father's Unspoken Words

In the silence of the prison walls, countless fathers carry within them unsent letters that weigh heavy on their hearts. These letters, filled with words of longing, regret, and love, are trapped within their minds, unable to find their way to the ones they are meant for. The stamp and envelope remain untouched, for the fathers do not know how to send them, leaving their children without the solace of their words.

As a result, a chasm forms between father and child, fueled by the absence of communication, the void of understanding. The child is left to navigate a world without the guidance and presence of their father, harboring resentment and anger towards the one who is physically absent but emotionally present.

America, we are called to address this brokenness, to mend the fractured relationships that stem from incarceration. The unspoken words of fathers must find a way to reach their children to bridge the gap that separates them. We must offer support and resources to enable incarcerated fathers to communicate with their children to express their remorse, their love, their longing for reconciliation.

Let us not allow these unspoken words to fester and breed further discord and pain. Let us create pathways for healing, for understanding, for forgiveness. Only then can we begin to mend the wounds of broken relationships to foster a sense of connection and belonging that transcends the barriers of incarceration.

May these unspoken words find their voice, and may they be heard, and be received with open hearts. May we strive to build a future where father and child are united in love, understanding, and healing.

Together, let us embark on this journey of reconciliation and restoration.

With hope and determination,

A Call for Change

Chapter 22:
The Role of the Church: Embracing Prodigal Families - Unity in Diversity (Luke 15:20)

In the intricate tapestry of our society, the nation of Yahweh, the churches, and the Islamic prison communities stand as pillars of support and transformation for prodigal families. Despite their differences in beliefs and practices, they are united in their mission to embrace and uplift those in need, especially the fatherless in our communities.

As these diverse groups come together, they recognize the urgent need to address the brokenness caused by absent fathers and the impact it has on families. They understand that the role of the man as the head of the household is crucial in providing stability, guidance, and love to their children.

Within the walls of the prison, a remarkable transformation takes place as men from all walks of life, including those who entered at a young age, have served decades behind bars. Despite their past mistakes and the years lost, they have grown and matured into responsible, caring individuals through the guidance of their faith and the support of their communities.

These men, like yourself, have found solace and strength in surrendering themselves to their higher power, allowing them to embrace their true calling as fathers and role models. The stories of redemption and change within the prison walls serve as a beacon of hope and inspiration to others, showcasing the transformative power of faith and community support.

Through countless examples of embracing and empowering individuals from diverse backgrounds, these groups demonstrate that regardless of one's past or circumstances, everyone has the potential to change, to grow, and to become the father, leader, and caregiver they were meant to be.

In the spirit of unity and understanding, let us continue to support and celebrate the journey of transformation and redemption for all individuals seeking a second chance, a new beginning, and a path toward healing and restoration.

Together, we can create a more compassionate and inclusive society where every individual, regardless of their past, is embraced, supported, and empowered to fulfill their potential as fathers, mentors, and pillars of strength in their families and communities.

With unity and love,

Embracing Prodigal Families

Chapter 23:
Community Transformation - Empowering Fathers and Homes (Isaiah 58:12)

In the vast landscape of the Florida Department of Correctional Institutions, a profound movement is unfolding - a movement where fathers imprisoned behind cold walls are finding strength, purpose, and redemption. Their voices, once muted and overlooked, are now rising with a message of hope, transformation, and empowerment.

Guided by Yahweh and the Jack Brewer Hero's Second Chance Movement, these fathers are not merely undergoing personal change; they are becoming catalysts for a new narrative of grace and renewal within their communities. Their stories are living proof of the resilience, faith, and determination that can lead to a brighter future.

As these fathers reclaim their roles as leaders and caregivers, they are not only reshaping their own destinies but also creating a ripple effect of change and inspiration in their surroundings. Their journey serves as a beacon of light, illuminating the path toward reconciliation, forgiveness, and second chances.

Community leaders are urged to bear witness to this transformation - to see the beauty and potential within these individuals who have experienced the touch of divine grace. It is time for communities to embrace these fathers, learn from their stories, and join hands with them in building a more compassionate and inclusive society.

Through their unwavering faith and dedication, these inmates are rewriting the narrative of fatherhood, masculinity, and community involvement. Their impact transcends prison walls, motivating others to believe in the power of transformation and the promise of new beginnings.

As we observe the remarkable work happening within correctional facilities, let us be moved to support and uplift these fathers as they write the next chapter of their lives and inspire others to do the same.

Drawing from the wisdom of Isaiah 58:12 in the King James Version - "And they that shall be of thee shall build the old waste places: thou shalt raise up the foundations of many generations; and thou shalt be called, the repairer of the breach, The restorer of paths to dwell in" - let us understand that the past, present, and future are intertwined in a journey of restoration, rebuilding, and healing.

Together, let us celebrate the journey of redemption, the triumph of the human spirit, and the enduring power of faith in transforming lives and communities for the better.

In unity and optimism,

Empowering Fathers and Homes

Chapter 24:
Fulfilling the Prophecy - A Vision for Restoration (Hosea 4:6)

The journey of restoration and transformation starts with acknowledging the harsh realities faced by incarcerated fathers, whose voices have been silenced by the walls of the prison system. This chapter aims to shed light on the plight of these men, who are often viewed by the government as mere numbers rather than the human beings, fathers, sons, and husbands they truly are. As we embark on this chapter, we must recognize that the path to restoration is not about denying the wrongs committed but rather about recognizing the immense potential for change and growth within these individuals.

The Transformation Within:

Throughout this book, we have explored the stories of men who, despite the challenges of incarceration, have embarked on a profound journey of personal transformation. These individuals, once lost to the system, have found purpose, redemption, and a renewed sense of identity through their faith, mentorship, and unwavering determination to better themselves.

Statistical Insights:

In the state of Florida, the statistics paint a sobering picture. A significant number of men currently incarcerated have been behind bars since their teenage years, some for over 30 years. These prolonged sentences, often driven by a system more concerned with punishment than rehabilitation, have robbed these individuals of the opportunity to fully embrace their roles as fathers, partners, and contributing members of society.

A Shift in Perspective:

However, a remarkable shift is taking place. A growing number of these incarcerated men have become God-fearing individuals, mentored by their fellow inmates who have walked a similar path. This grassroots movement of change, fueled by a deeper understanding of faith and personal accountability, stands in stark contrast to the narrative often perpetuated by society. It is a testament to the resilience of the human spirit and the power of community-driven transformation.

The Guiding Light:

In this context, individuals like Jake Brewer and his dedicated team have become beacons of hope, offering unwavering support and mentorship to these men. Their commitment to remembering their brothers, even in the face of societal indifference, has been a driving force in the lives of those seeking redemption. This book, which has taken shape through the collaborative efforts of Ricky, Dakota, and the author, is a testament to the transformative power of faith, community, and the unwavering belief in the capacity for change.

Conclusion:

As we conclude this chapter, we stand at the cusp of a profound transformation. The men who have walked through the gates of the prison system are no longer the same individuals who entered. They are fathers, sons, and husbands who have found the strength to break the cycle, reclaim their identities, and become agents of positive change within their communities. It is time for society to recognize this transformation and embrace the restoration that lies within these individuals, fulfilling the prophecy of Hosea 4:6 and paving the way for a future where the incarcerated are seen not as numbers but as human beings worthy of redemption.

A Closing Call to Action

As we come to the end of this transformative journey, I would like to express my deepest gratitude to all who have traversed these pages with open hearts and minds. This work has been a sacred calling, guided by the hand of the divine, and your willingness to engage with its message has been truly humbling.

Throughout these chapters, we have borne witness to the profound stories of redemption and restoration – tales of individuals who, once lost in the cycles of brokenness and incarceration, have emerged as beacons of hope, their renewed mindsets shining a path forward for both themselves and their communities.

As we reflect on the lessons imparted within these pages, let us not forget the rippling impact of incarceration – the way in which the loss of freedom does not merely affect the individual but the entire family structure. It is a painful reality that too often goes overlooked, leaving the bonds of kinship shattered and the wounds of separation slow to heal.

Yet, it is within this very realization that we find the seeds of a more compassionate, restorative approach to justice and societal reintegration, for it is only by acknowledging the collateral damage of incarceration and actively working to facilitate the reunification and healing of families that we can begin to truly address the root causes of societal dysfunction.

I therefore call upon you, the readers, to heed the clarion call of these transformed individuals – to open your hearts and minds to their stories, to provide them with the platforms and support they need to share their wisdom, and to actively engage in the creation of systems that prioritize restoration over mere punishment.

For in doing so, we not only empower the formerly incarcerated but also inspire those who are still struggling, offering a beacon of hope and a pathway toward reconciliation and wholeness. It is through this collective effort, this shared commitment to compassion and justice, that we can begin to heal the deep-seated wounds that have plagued our communities for far too long.

May the divine continue to guide us in this sacred mission, and may the words and actions that flow from this book serve as a rallying cry for a more just, equitable, and restorative future – one in which the dignity of every individual is honored, and the power of redemption is celebrated as a testament to the boundless potential of the human spirit.

Samuel Ben Israel's Story

Dear brother of mine, who still finds himself behind the prison walls at a Correctional Institution alongside me, allow me to share with you the inspiring story of a man I know well - Samuel Ben Israel. He is not just a brother and a close friend but also a mentor and elder in the community of the Nation of Yahweh, a true leader in every sense of the word.

Samuel's journey began in the 11th ward of New Orleans, a low-income section known for its hardships. Growing up with just his mother and siblings, Samuel faced challenges that shaped his path in profound ways. Inside his own mind, back in those days, Samuel had dreams and ideals for his life, but the realities of his environment often clouded those aspirations. It seemed like time moved differently for him. Each year felt like two years as he took on responsibilities beyond his years.

By the age of ten, Samuel was already seen as a grown man by many, shouldering the burden of providing for himself in the absence of a father figure. Despite his mother's love and support, the influence of the impoverished environment led him astray, engaging in risky behaviors like smoking weed, stealing cars, and other unlawful activities. The allure of street life dimmed his once bright dreams, and by the time he was fifteen, now known as Skully, he found himself entrenched in a world of crime and recklessness.

But it was a turning point, a pivotal moment when Yahweh intervened in Samuel's life. Despite facing a death sentence, an encounter with an older inmate on death row planted seeds of faith in his heart, leading him to discover a new purpose and direction. Embracing Yahweh as his guide and father, Samuel's life took on a transformative path.

Released to serve a life sentence in a Florida prison, Samuel became a beacon of hope and spirituality among his fellow inmates. His unwavering faith and wisdom inspired those around him, showing them the power of Yahweh's love and guidance. Today, Samuel stands as one of the greatest spiritual leaders I've ever encountered, despite not ever having a father figure. As he often reminds us, there is no greater father than Yahweh.

May Samuel's story serve as a testament to the power of faith, redemption, and the transformative work of Yahweh in our lives. Let his example continue to guide us as we navigate through our own journey behind these prison walls.

Let us come together to lift up prayers for our dear brother, Samuel Ben Israel, who has devoted his life to prayer and guidance for others. Let us beseech Yahweh to grant him release to be reunited with his family soon. Dear brother, know that you are loved and appreciated for your unwavering commitment to Yahweh's path.

Thank you for your dedication and submission to Yahweh's will, dear brother. The Holy Spirit works through you, touching and transforming countless lives within these walls. Keep up the good work of spreading Yahweh's love and light, for you are truly a beacon of hope and inspiration in our midst. May Yahweh continue to guide and bless you in all your endeavors.

Jacoby Ben Israel's Bio

My name is Jacoby Ben Israel, and I'm an inmate currently serving time at a Correctional Institution. I am 38 years old and grew up in a single-parent home with my mother, Mary Martin, and my three brothers and seven sisters. Looking back, that was just too much responsibility for one mother to handle, trying to raise a family of 11 kids in a low-income environment.

At a very young age, I was introduced to a life of crime – stealing, robbing, and selling drugs. In my young, misguided mind, I told myself that I was doing this to help provide for my mother and our large family. I was driven by greed, selfishness, and a complete disregard for the well-being of others. My unrighteous mindset led me down a dark path, and before long, I found myself sentenced to life in prison for my actions.

At the time, I was unapologetic and convinced that I was above the law. I had no remorse for the harm I had caused, only a single-minded focus on what I perceived as taking care of my family. Little did I know this was just the beginning of a profound transformation that would take place over the course of my incarceration.

When I first came to prison back in 2005, I was still living by the same principles and engaging in the same criminal behavior that had landed me here in the first place. Every single day, my unrighteous way of living had me facing problem after problem within the prison system. I was trapped in a vicious cycle of selfishness and disregard for the law.

It wasn't until 2014 that a good brother from Fort Myers, a homeboy named Johnny Truesdale, also known as JT, came into my life. That brother planted a seed by enlightening me about Yahweh.

From that point on, a profound transformation began to take place within me.

I started to question the values and beliefs that had once defined me. A newfound sense of morality began to emerge as I dedicated myself to personal growth and rehabilitation. I realized the weight of my past actions and the consequences of the choices I had made. The isolation and solitude of incarceration forced me to confront my own shortcomings and the harm I had caused.

Through this journey of self-discovery, I came to recognize the error of my ways. I made a conscious decision to turn my life around and live by moral principles, seeking to atone for my past transgressions. This awakening marked the beginning of my redemption, a testament to the power of the human spirit to overcome even the darkest of circumstances.

Since I came into the knowledge of God Yahweh and genuinely connected with my inner self, I have discovered my purpose in life. Despite the life sentence imposed by man for my past actions, Yahweh has granted me freedom and eternal life through his son. This spiritual awakening has opened my eyes to a higher calling.

I now understand that my purpose is to serve and help others in any way I can. I have realized that by humbling myself and allowing Yahweh's presence to be seen through my actions, I can make a positive impact on those around me. Finding peace in giving back to all people, regardless of their color or beliefs, has become my mission.

I firmly believe that there is only one God who unites us all. In my journey of mentoring others, I strive to ensure they are given the same chance for redemption and transformation that I received. Through acts of kindness, guidance, and support, I aim to spread the message of love and compassion that Yahweh has instilled in me. My past may have been marked by darkness, but I am now dedicated to shining a light of hope and inspiration for those in need.

I would like to extend a special thanks to the Jack Brewer Foundation for bringing men of like minds together. It is through this unity that we can see that, no matter how we believe or practice our faith, we can achieve the same goals. Our shared mission to be impactful fathers in our children's lives transcends any differences and unites us in a common purpose.

Hezekiah Ben Israel's Story

I walk these prison grounds at a Correctional Institution in the Florida Department of Correction with these incredible men, praying for redemption and a second chance. It is a cause that is deeply personal to me, as I have witnessed firsthand the transformative power of faith and rehabilitation.

My thoughts drift to my dear friend Hezekiah Ben Israel, who had once been a pillar of our community. Ronald, a devoted father of six, found solace in his faith in Yahweh, dedicating his life to serving others. But a fateful arrest in 2014 had shattered his world, leaving him facing a 70-year prison sentence.

At the time of his arrest, Ronald was 34 years old, but he is now 43 and will be 44 on July 15th. As I bow my head, I plead with the higher power I serve, Yahweh, to open the eyes of the justice system. "How can we allow our brothers, our sons, and our fathers to be separated from their families for so long, with no remedy for the positive change they've shown? "I whisper, my voice heavy with emotion.

I know that Ronald is not the same man who had once made those mistakes that landed him in this predicament. Through his unwavering commitment to Yahweh, he has transformed himself, becoming a beacon of hope and guidance for others. Yet, the system seems unwilling to recognize this redemption, trapping Ronald behind bars and robbing his children of their father's love and presence.

The men around me join me in prayer, our collective voices rising to the heavens, asking for compassion, understanding, and a reevaluation of the way society treats those who have served their time and proven their dedication to a better future.

"We cannot turn a blind eye to the power of change," I declare, my eyes shining with determination. "These men, like Ronald, deserve a second chance, a chance to reunite with their families and continue their journey of redemption. Yahweh, Jesus, Allah: whomever you call unto, hear our plea and guide us towards a more just and merciful justice system."

As the prayer service comes to a close, my heart is filled with a renewed sense of purpose. I know that the road ahead will be long and arduous, but I am willing to be a voice for the forgotten, to fight for the families torn apart by the harsh realities of the justice system, for in the end, it is not just about Hezekiah Ben Israel or any one individual – it is about restoring the humanity and dignity that every person deserves, no matter their previous transgressions or past.

Hezekiah Ben Israel's Bio

As I embark on recounting my life's journey, I am reminded of the tumultuous path that has shaped me into who I am today. Each chapter unfolds a tale of triumphs and tribulations, a series of events that have left an indelible mark on my soul.

Early Years (Age 5-7)

The echo of screeching tires and shattering glass still reverberates in my mind from the day of my mother's accident. With her amnesia robbing her of recognition, my sisters and I were thrust into a world of confusion and isolation. Our grandmother's subsequent passing orphaned us at a tender age, casting us adrift in a sea of uncertainty.

Foster Care and Identity Crisis (Age 7-12)

Foster care became a labyrinth of instability and turmoil as I found myself tossed between unfamiliar homes, yearning for a sense of belonging. I fought fiercely to shield my sisters, only to be torn apart from them in the end. Lost in an identity crisis, I sought solace in the refuge of school despite the shadows of bullying and discrimination that clouded my days.

In the years of my life between the age of 13 and 18, the weight of iron bars and the chill of prison walls have become my constant companions, a harsh reminder of the sacrifice I made to protect my family. Despite the suffocating confines, my spirit remains unbroken as I navigate the harsh realities of the justice system. Through the darkness, I draw strength from my unyielding faith and the unwavering support of my loved ones.

Within the confines of incarceration, I have faced myriad obstacles, from brutal assaults to heartbreaking betrayals. Yet, amidst the shadows of despair, glimmers of hope and redemption have emerged. I have seized opportunities to achieve personal growth, earning my GED, acquiring new skills, and offering guidance to fellow inmates. My journey stands as a testament to the resilience of the human spirit in overcoming adversity.

My story echoes a poignant plea for reform, a call to arms for justice, second chances, and the rights of those silenced by inequality. Together, let us forge a world where freedom and redemption are not distant dreams but tangible realities.

From the depths of my cell, I have beheld the unwavering resilience inherent in the human spirit. Despite the adversities that beset us, hope remains steadfast, illuminating the path towards freedom and liberation.

Family, a beacon of unwavering support and unconditional love has been my rock through the tumultuous waves of life. In my daughter, Rhoniyah, I find solace and strength, a driving force that propels me forward in the face of adversity.

The repercussions of incarceration extend far beyond prison walls, resonating deeply within the hearts of loved ones and the community. I refuse to be defined by this experience but seek to transform it into a catalyst for positive change.

To those who have walked alongside me through the pages of my narrative, I implore you to take a stand. Champion criminal justice reform, support initiatives aiding the incarcerated, and above all, believe in the transformative power of redemption.

As I inscribe these words, a glimmer of hope lights the way to a fresh beginning. With the promise of freedom on the horizon, I carry within me the fervent belief that my story will kindle a flame of resilience and inspire others never to relinquish hope.

Freedom transcends mere words; it embodies the sensation of renewal, of vitality, of love rekindled. This precious gift, once attained, shall be treasured eternally.

My journey stands as a testament to the triumph of the human spirit amidst adversity, a testament to the enduring quest for justice, freedom, and the amplification of silenced voices in the tumult of injustice. I am not merely a statistic, not merely an inmate—I am a human being, resolute in my pursuit of justice and redemption for all those marginalized by the system.

Reflecting on the chapters of my tumultuous odyssey, I am compelled by the myriad souls still ensnared in the clutches of the system, yearning for a second chance, a glimmer of hope. While I may not alter the past, together, we can sculpt a future imbued with justice in its truest form.

Should you be a legal advocate, a proponent of justice, or simply a believer in righteousness, I beseech you to unite in this crusade. Let us unite in dismantling the existing status quo, questioning the system, and fashioning a realm where justice permeates every fiber of existence.

Your perusal of my chronicle is a testament to your belief in me; let us forge ahead together, ardently striving for a world where equity reigns supreme.

I extend my deepest gratitude for delving into the tapestry of my life. Thank you for standing by me and for having faith in the possibility of justice. Together, let us wage a valiant struggle for a future brimming with equity and illumination for all.

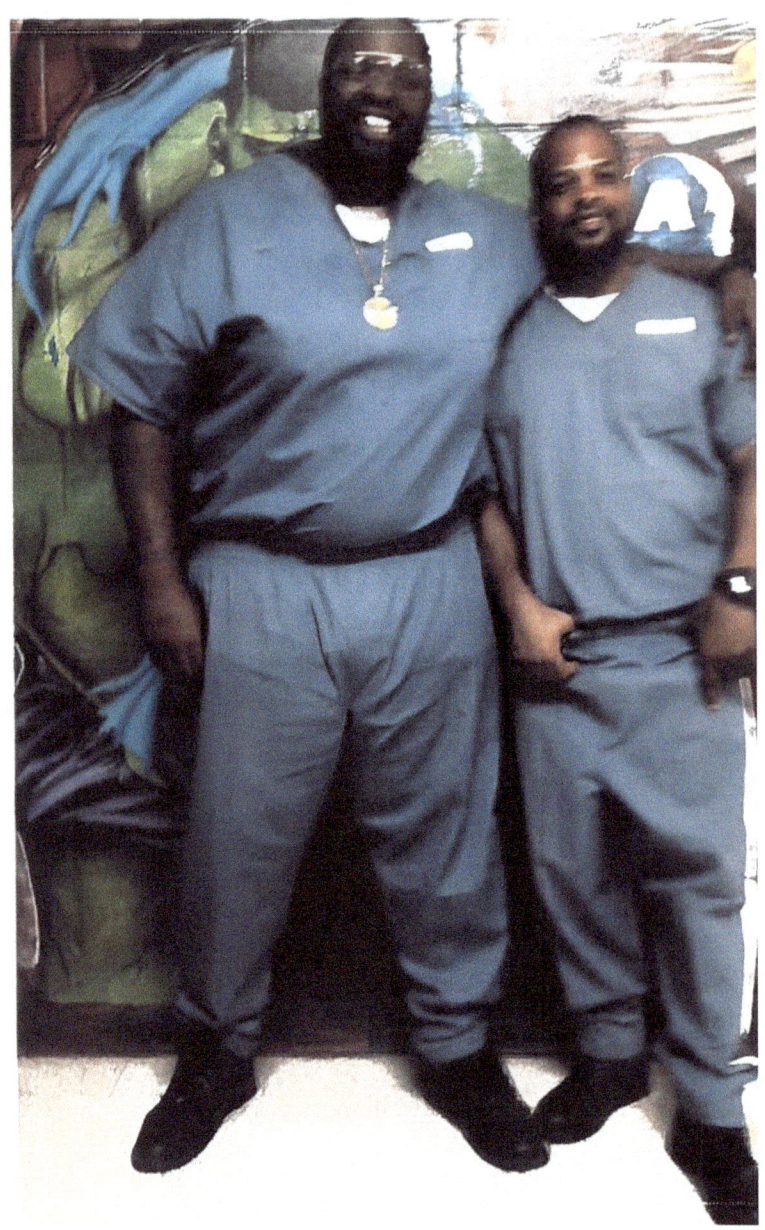

Yarah Ben Israel & Samuel Ben Israel

Author's Note

As I bring this profound journey to a close, my heart overflows with deep gratitude to the guiding hand of my creator, Yahweh. It is through the grace and wisdom of the Holy Spirit that I have been entrusted as a messenger, a vessel through which transformative words and ideas have flowed.

To my beloved wife, Terri Brown, I offer my deepest thanks. Your unwavering support, your relentless pushing, and your belief in my potential have been the driving forces that have propelled me forward, leaving me no choice but to succeed. I am forever grateful for your love and commitment.

My cherished daughters, Qeasha Hill and Dr. Dre, and my precious, brilliant grandbaby Leah - your presence in my life has been a wellspring of joy and inspiration. You are the reasons why I continue to strive, grow, and create a better world.

To my brothers behind these prison walls, I salute you. Your mentorship, your embrace of change, and your dedication to becoming better fathers have been a constant source of motivation and hope. Together, we have weathered the storms of incarceration, emerging stronger and more resolute in our faith.

And to all my brothers through Yahweh, near and far, know that I feel your love and pride. We have walked this path of transformation side by side, supporting one another, and I am honored to call you family.

To those whose names may not have been mentioned, please understand that your presence, your contributions, and your steadfast support have not gone unnoticed. You are all woven into the tapestry of this journey, and your impact is felt deeply within these pages.

I would also like to extend my heartfelt gratitude to the Jake Brewer Second Chance Initiative Foundation. Your unwavering commitment to providing opportunities and resources for the formerly incarcerated has been a beacon of hope, and I am honored to be a part of your noble endeavors.

As we part ways, I urge you all to remain steadfast in your faith, to place your trust in Yahweh, and to continue on the path of redemption and restoration, for it is only through the unwavering embrace of the divine that we can truly overcome the challenges that lie before us and emerge as beacons of hope for ourselves, our families, and our communities.

May the words and deeds that have been birthed from this sacred work continue to ripple outward, touching the lives of all who encounter them. And may the spirit of Yahweh guide us, strengthen us, and inspire us to create a world where justice, compassion, and the power of transformation reign supreme.

With love and gratitude,

John Brown (Yarah Ben Israel)

Co-Author's Note

I am Samuel Ben Israel, and I first want to express my deepest gratitude to my God, Yahweh, with whom I share a very personal relationship. I am forever thankful for His guidance and blessings throughout my journey.

I also want to dedicate this note to my Queen, Toni, whose love and unwavering support serve as a beacon of hope in my life. Toni, I love you with all my heart.

A special thank you goes out to my family, who have been my pillars of strength and support. Your love and encouragement have fueled my determination to strive for better each day. I am especially grateful to my mother and mother-in-law for their strength and unwavering belief in me.

To all of Israel, shalom achs. I am inspired by the faith and perseverance of my brothers, who believe in the unseen and continue to strive for greatness. Your dedication motivates me to keep pushing forward.

I want to send a message of solidarity and love to my brothers at any Correctional Institution. This is for you – South Who! Let's continue to work towards a better future, knowing that God has a plan for each of us.

To my brothers at South Bay Correctional and all other institutions across Florida, let us raise our voices and stand united. Together, we can make a difference and bring about positive change.

I invite you to join the Unshackled Voices of Incarcerated Fathers movement and the Jack Brewer Foundation Second Chance Heroes movement. These movements seek to rebuild fractured homes, break generational curses, and keep future generations out of the cycle of incarceration.

For those who wish to learn more or get involved, please reach out to our team at:

Unshackled Voices <unshacklevoices@gmail.com>

Unshackled voices of Incarcerated fathers:

P.O. Box 51565

Ft. Myers, Florida

Thank you to everyone who supports our cause. Your love and dedication are truly appreciated.

With love and respect,

Samuel Ben Israel.